MASTER YOUR MIND!

T0144936

The Condensed Classics Bundles Library

INFINITE MIND POWER
LEADERSHIP
MASTER YOUR MIND!
MONEY MAGIC!
NAPOLEON HILL'S GOLDEN CLASSICS
SUCCESS DYNAMITE
SUCCESS SECRETS OF THE GREAT MASTERS
THE POWER OF OPTIMISM

MASTER YOUR MIND!

JOSEPH MURPHY
*The Power of Your
Subconscious Mind*

JAMES ALLEN
As a Man Thinketh

FLORENCE SCOVEL SHINN
The Game of Life

ABRIDGED AND INTRODUCED BY
MITCH HOROWITZ

Published by Gildan Media LLC
aka G&D Media.
www.GandDmedia.com

The Power of Your Subconscious Mind was originally published in 1963
As a Man Thinketh was originally published in 1903
The Game of Life and How to Play It was originally published in 1925
G&D Media Condensed Classics edition published 2018
Abridgement and Introduction copyright © 2015, 2018 by Mitch Horowitz

FIRST EDITION: 2018

Cover design by David Rheinhardt of Pyrographx

Interior design by Meghan Day Healey of Story Horse, LLC.

ISBN: 978-1-7225-0090-0

Contents

Introduction
vii

THE POWER OF YOUR SUBCONSCIOUS MIND
1

AS A MAN THINKETH
51

THE GAME OF LIFE
103

Introduction

The Power of *Maybe*
By Mitch Horowitz

Sometimes I attempt a personal experiment, which I invite you to join me in. I approach a favorite or perennial book of mind metaphysics and attempt to free myself of all preconceptions surrounding it or its ideas; and I ask: How would these ideas affect me if I were encountering them for the very first time? If I were trying them with a completely fresh mind? The results can be remarkable.

I ask you to adopt that same spirit as you approach the three condensed classics in this collection: *The Power of Your Subconscious Mind* by Joseph Murphy; *As a Man Thinketh* by James Allen, and *The Game of Life* by Florence Scovel Shinn.

Although each writer in *Master Your Mind!* differs in tone and emphasis, all agree on one core point: *your thoughts are your destiny.* I believe in this principle, even though I have also noted that we live under many laws and forces—of which the mind is one vital component.

Introduction

I have always loved the popular literature of mind metaphysics. These three works are prime examples of how this kind of writing imbues its reader with a sense of *practical possibility*. Many remarkable things can emerge from a feeling of possibility. Philosopher William James (1842-1910)—himself an avid experimenter in mind metaphysics—called it the sense of "maybe." James wrote this in his 1895 essay *Is Life Worth Living?*:

> The "scientific" life itself has much to do with maybes, and human life at large has everything to do with them. So far as man stands for anything, and is productive or originative at all, his entire vital function may be said to be to deal with maybes. Not a victory is gained, not a deed of faithfulness or courage is done, except upon a maybe . . . It is only by risking our persons from one hour to another that we live at all. And often enough our faith beforehand in an uncertified result is the only thing that makes the result come true. Suppose, for instance, that you are climbing a mountain and have worked yourself into a position from which the only escape is by a terrible leap. Have faith that you can successfully make it, and your feet are nerved to its accomplishment. But mistrust yourself, and think of all the sweet

things you have heard the scientists say of maybes, and you will hesitate so that, at last, all unstrung and trembling, and launching yourself in a moment of despair, you roll in the abyss. In such a case (and it belongs to an enormous class), the part of wisdom as well as of courage is to believe what is in the line of your needs, for only by the belief is the need fulfilled.

This is as good a reason as I've ever found to experiment with the kinds of ideas you'll encounter in this book. James often noted that *belief* in something—including Deity itself—may be the determining factor as how or whether you experience its effects in your life. By *effects*, James meant that which is concretely measurable in behavior and experience. Hence, your belief in the actualizing power of your mental images and thoughts can, in itself, increase their efficacy.

That is the possibility this guidebook holds open for you. *Master Your Mind!* exposes you to some of the best, most practical, and most persuasive ideas about the generative powers of thought. It is, in short, a remarkable experiment awaiting your participation. As I write these words, I am eager and joyful for you as to what you may find.

THE POWER
OF YOUR
SUBCONSCIOUS
MIND

THE POWER
OF YOUR
SUBCONSCIOUS
MIND

by Joseph Murphy

The Original Classic

Abridged and Introduced
by Mitch Horowitz

THE CONDENSED CLASSICS LIBRARY™

Contents

Introduction
The Power of Thought.....................................9

Chapter One
The Treasure House Within You...............13

Chapter Two
How Your Mind Works 15

Chapter Three
The Miracle-Working Power
of Your Subconscious Mind 17

Chapter Four
Prayer and Your Subconscious Mind........ 19

Chapter Five
How to Get the Results You Want............ 23

CHAPTER SIX

How to Use Your
Subconscious Mind for Wealth 25

CHAPTER SEVEN

Your Subconscious Mind
as a Partner in Career Success 29

CHAPTER EIGHT

The Inventiveness of
Your Subconscious Mind 31

CHAPTER NINE

Your Subconscious Mind
and Marital Problems 33

CHAPTER TEN

Your Subconscious Mind
and Happiness 37

CHAPTER ELEVEN

Your Subconscious Mind
and Harmonious Relationships 39

CHAPTER TWELVE

How Your Subconscious Mind Removes Mental Blocks 43

CHAPTER THIRTEEN

How to Stay Young in Spirit Forever 47

ABOUT THE AUTHORS 49

The Power of Thought

This may be one of the most personally important books you ever encounter. I say that not because I agree with every one of its premises or ideas. But, rather, because author and New Thought minister Joseph Murphy identifies and expands upon one immensely important and undervalued principle: *What you think dramatically affects your quality of life.*

This idea has been restated from antiquity to the present. John Milton put it this way in *Paradise Lost*: "The mind is its own place, and in it self can make a Heav'n of Hell, a Hell of Heav'n."

Murphy presents this principle as an absolute. He argues that thought governs health, finances, relationships, and all facets of life. I am personally unconvinced that *every* element of existence yields to thought alone. But within the folds of this idea—that mind is the master builder—can be found great truths. They are yours to discover, test, and benefit from. All that is required is to change how you think.

Murphy's philosophy is profoundly simple—but it is not for the weak or myopic. If you take seriously what you find in this book—and I urge you to—you will discover that redirecting your thoughts toward resiliency and constructiveness requires a lifetime of effort. But it is a task worthy of every motivated, mature person.

You will also learn that your emotions must be brought into play for any real self-change to occur. Emotion is more powerful than thought—never confuse or conflate the two. The mind says, "be satisfied with your portion"—emotion shouts, "I want more!" The mind says, "be calm"—emotion wants to run away. The mind says, "I'm happy for my neighbor"—emotion feels envy. Murphy supplies exercises to help align your emotions and thoughts in pursuit of a personal goal.

Murphy's message that *new thought means new life* has touched countless people since this book first appeared in 1963. This is not because Murphy's outlook is cloying or wishful; but because it is essentially true. We *all* feel that we should be practicing more dignified, generous, and self-respecting patterns of thought, tones of speech, and person-to-person relations. We harbor the conviction that we are *not* leading the lives we should be—that our abilities are underdeveloped, our decisions too hesitant and timorous, and our attitudes too selfish. Almost all of us sense the potential of a larger existence within us. This is a near-universal instinct.

The Power of Your Subconscious Mind is an instruction manual toward seeking that greater scale of life. Pay close attention to the book's principles, methods, and exercises. And, above all, *use them*.

It may be the most important step you ever take.

—Mitch Horowitz

CHAPTER ONE

The Treasure House Within You

What, in your opinion, is the master secret of the ages? Atomic power? Thermonuclear energy? Interplanetary travel? No—not any of these. What, then, is the master secret? Where can one find it, and how can it be contacted and brought into action? The answer is extraordinarily simple. The secret is the marvelous, miracle-working power of your own subconscious mind.

You can bring into your life more ability, more health, more wealth, and more happiness by learning to contact and release the hidden forces of your subconscious.

As you follow the simple techniques in this book, you can gain the necessary knowledge and understanding to unlock your subconscious depths. Within them are infinite wisdom, infinite power, and infinite supply. Begin now to recognize these potentialities of your deeper mind, and they will take form in the world without.

The infinite intelligence within your subconscious can reveal to you everything you need to know at every moment, provided you are open-minded and receptive. You can receive new thoughts and ideas enabling you to bring forth new inventions, make new discoveries, or write plays and books. You can attract the ideal companion. You can acquire resources and wealth. You can move forward in abundance, security, joy, and dominion.

It is your *right* to discover this inner world of thought. Its miracle-working powers and eternal laws of life existed before you were born, before any religion or church appeared, and before the world itself came into being. It is with these thoughts that I urge you in the following chapters to lay hold of this wonderful, magical, transforming power that is your subconscious mind.

How Your Mind Works

There are two levels of mind, conscious and subconscious. You think with your rational, conscious mind—and whatever you habitually think seeps down into your subconscious mind, which creates according to the nature of your thoughts.

Once the subconscious mind accepts an idea, it begins to execute it. Your subconscious does not engage in *proving* whether your thoughts are good or bad, but responds according to the *nature* of your thoughts or suggestions. If you consciously assume something is true, even though it may be false, your subconscious will accept it and proceed to bring about results that must necessarily follow.

Your conscious mind is the "watchman at the gate." Its chief function is to protect your subconscious from false impressions. You now know one of the basic laws of mind: Your subconscious is amenable to *suggestion*.

From infancy on, many of us have been given negative suggestions. Not knowing how to thwart them, we unconsciously accepted them. Here are some of the negative suggestions: "You can't." "You'll never amount to anything." "You'll fail." "You haven't got a chance." "It's no use." "It's not what you know, but who you know." "You're too old now." And so on.

If you look back, you can easily recall how parents, friends, relatives, teachers, and associates contributed to a campaign of negative suggestions. Study the things said to you, and you will discover that much of it was said to control you or instill fear in you. Check regularly on the negative suggestions that people make to you today. You do not have to be influenced by destructive suggestion.

Never say: "I can't." Overcome fear of failure by substituting the following statement: *I can do all things through the power of my subconscious mind.*

Never allow others to think for you. Choose your own thoughts, and make your own decisions. Always remember that *you have the capacity to choose.* Choose life! Choose love! Choose health! Choose happiness! Whatever your conscious mind assumes and believes, your subconscious mind accepts and brings to pass.

Chapter Three

The Miracle-Working Power of Your Subconscious Mind

The power of your subconscious mind is enormous. It inspires you, guides you, and reveals to you names, facts, and scenes from the storehouse of memory.

Your subconscious mind never sleeps or rests. You can discover its miracle-working power by plainly stating to your subconscious prior to sleep that you wish to accomplish a certain thing. You will be delighted to find that forces within you will be released, leading to the desired answer or result.

William James, the father of American psychology, said that the power to move the world resides within your subconscious mind. Your subconscious is at one with infinite intelligence and boundless wisdom. It is fed by hidden springs. The law of life operates through it. Whatever you impress upon your subconscious, it will move heaven and earth to bring it to pass. You must, therefore, impress it with right ideas and constructive thoughts.

What is your idea or feeling about yourself right now? Every part of your being expresses that idea. Your body, vitality, finances, friends, and social status are a perfect reflection of the idea you have of yourself. What is impressed in your subconscious mind is expressed in all phases of your life.

Worry, anxiety, and fear can interfere with the normal rhythm of your heart, lungs, and other organs. Feed your subconscious mind with thoughts of harmony, health, and peace, and all the functions of your body will become normal again.

Feel the thrill of accomplishment, imagine the happy ending or solution to your problem, and what you imagine and feel will be accepted by your subconscious mind and brought to pass. The life principle will flow through you rhythmically and harmoniously as you consciously affirm: *I believe that the subconscious power that gave me this desire is now fulfilling it through me.*

Your subconscious mind can and will accomplish as much as you allow it to.

CHAPTER FOUR

Prayer and Your Subconscious Mind

I n building the Golden Gate Bridge, the chief engineer understood mathematical principles, stresses, and strains. Secondly, he had a picture of the ideal bridge across the bay. The third step was his application of tried and proven methods, which were implemented until the bridge took form. Likewise, there exist techniques and methods by which your prayers are actualized.

Prayer is the formulation of an idea concerning something you wish to accomplish. Your desire *is* your prayer. It comes out of your deepest needs and it reveals what you want in life. *Blessed are they that hunger and thirst after righteousness: for they shall be filled.* That is really prayer: life's hunger and thirst for peace, harmony, health, joy, and other blessings.

We will now explore the "passing over" technique for impregnating the subconscious mind with your desire. This involves inducing the subconscious to *take over* your prayer request as handed it by the conscious mind. This *passing over* is best accomplished in a reverie-like state. Know that within your deeper mind exist infinite intelligence and infinite power. Just calmly think over what you want; and see it coming into fuller fruition from this moment forward.

Your prayer—*your mental act*—must be accepted as an image in your mind before the power of your subconscious will play upon it and make it operative. You must reach a point of *acceptance* in your mind, an unqualified and undisputed state of agreement.

This contemplation should be accompanied by a feeling of joy and restfulness in foreseeing the accomplishment of your desire. The basis for the art and science of true prayer is your knowledge and complete confidence that the movement of your conscious mind will gain a definite response from your subconscious mind.

The easiest and most obvious way to formulate an idea is to visualize it, to see it in your mind's eye as vividly as if it were alive. You can see with the naked eye only what already exists in the external world; in a similar way, that which you can visualize in your mind's eye *already exists* in the infinite realms of thought. Any picture that you have in your mind is *the substance of things hoped for and the evidence of things not seen.* What you form in your imagination is as real as any part of your body.

Your ideas and thoughts are *real*—and will one day appear in the objective world if you remain faithful to your mental image.

Chapter Five

How to Get the Results You Want

The principle reasons for failure when trying to tap your subconscious are: 1) lack of confidence, and 2) too much effort.

Many people block answers to their prayers by failing to fully comprehend the nature of their subconscious. When you know how your mind functions, you gain a measure of *confidence*. You must remember that whenever your subconscious accepts an idea, it immediately begins to execute it. It uses all its mighty resources to that end, and mobilizes all the mental and spiritual faculties of your deeper mind. This law is true for good ideas or bad. Consequently, if you use it negatively, it brings trouble, failure, and confusion. When you use it constructively, it brings guidance, freedom, and peace.

The right answer is inevitable when your thoughts are constructive and loving. The only thing you have to do to overcome failure is to get your subconscious to accept your idea or request by *feeling its reality now*, and the law of your mind will do the rest. Turn over the request with faith and confidence, and your subconscious will take over and see it through.

You will always fail to get results by trying to use *mental coercion*—your subconscious does not respond to coercion; it responds to your faith or conscious-mind acceptance. Relaxation is the key. *Easy does it.* Do not be concerned with details and means, but rest in the assured end.

Feeling is the touchstone of all subconscious demonstration. Your new idea must be *felt subjectively*, not in the future but in a finished state, as coming about now. Get the *feel* of the happy solution to your problem. Remember how you felt in the past when you solved a major problem or recovered from a serious illness. Live in this feeling, and your subconscious depths will bring it to pass.

CHAPTER SIX

How to Use Your Subconscious Mind for Wealth

Wealth is a subconscious conviction on the part of the individual. You will not become a millionaire by saying, "I am a millionaire, I am a millionaire." Rather, you will *grow into a wealth consciousness* by building into your mentality the idea of wealth and abundance.

Perhaps you are saying to yourself now, "I need wealth and success." Follow these steps: Repeat for about five minutes to yourself three or four times a day, "Wealth—Success." These words have tremendous power. They represent the inner power of the subconscious. Anchor your mind on this substantial power within you; then corresponding conditions and circumstances will be manifested in your life.

Again, you are not merely saying, "I am wealthy." You are dwelling on real powers within you. There is no conflict in the mind when you say, "Wealth." Furthermore, the *feeling* of wealth will well up within you as you dwell on the idea of wealth.

I have talked to many people during the past thirty-five years whose usual complaint is: "I have said for weeks and months, 'I am wealthy, I am prosperous,' and nothing has happened." I discovered that when they said, "I am prosperous, I am wealthy," they felt within that they were lying to themselves. One man told me, "I have affirmed that I am prosperous until I am tired. Things are now worse. I knew when I made that statement that it was obviously not true." His statements were rejected by the conscious mind, and the very opposite of what he outwardly affirmed was made manifest.

Your affirmation succeeds best when it is specific and when it does not produce a mental conflict or argument; hence, the statements made by this man made matters worse because they suggested his lack. Your subconscious mind accepts what you really feel to be true, not just idle words or statements.

Here is the ideal way to overcome this conflict. Make this statement frequently, particularly prior to sleep: *By day and by night I am being prospered in all of my interests.* This affirmation will not arouse any argument because it does not contradict your subconscious mind's impression of financial lack.

Many people tell themselves, "I deserve a higher salary." I believe that most people are, in fact, underpaid. One reason why many people do not have more money is that they are silently or openly condemning it. They call money "filthy lucre" or say "love of money is the root of all evil." Another reason they do not prosper is that they have a sneaky subconscious feeling that there is some virtue in poverty. This subconscious pattern may be due to early childhood training, superstition, or a mistaken interpretation of Scripture

Cleanse your mind of all conflicting beliefs about money. Do not regard money as evil or filthy. If you do, you cause it to take wings and fly away from you. You lose what you condemn.

At the same time, do not make a god of money. It is only a symbol. Remember that the real riches are in your mind. You are here to lead a balanced life—and that includes acquiring all the money you need.

There is one emotion that causes lack of wealth in the lives of many. Most people learn this the hard way. It is envy. To entertain envious thoughts is devastating; it places you in a negative position in which wealth flows *from* you rather than *to* you. If you are ever annoyed or irritated by the prosperity of another, claim immediately that you truly wish him greater wealth in every possible way. This will neutralize your negative thoughts, and cause an ever-greater measure of wealth to flow to you.

CHAPTER SEVEN

Your Subconscious Mind as a Partner in Career Success

L et us discuss three steps to success. The first step is to discover the thing you love to do, and then do it. Success is in loving your work.

Some may say, "How can I put the first step into operation? I do not know what I should do." In such a case, pray for guidance as follows: *The infinite intelligence of my subconscious mind reveals to me my true place in life.* Repeat this prayer quietly, positively, and lovingly to your deeper mind. As you persist with faith and confidence, the answer will come to you as a feeling, a hunch, or a tendency in a certain direction. It will come to you clearly and in peace, as an inner awareness.

The second step to success is to specialize in some particular branch of work, and to know more about it than anyone else. For example, if a young man chooses chemistry as his profession, he should concentrate on one of the many branches in that field. He should give all of his time and attention to his chosen specialty. He should become sufficiently enthusiastic to know all there is about it; if possible, he should know more than anyone else.

The third step is the most important. You must be certain that the thing you want to do does not build your success only. *Your desire must not be selfish; it must benefit humanity.* The path of a complete circuit must be formed. In other words, your idea must go forth with the purpose of blessing or serving the world. It will then come back to you pressed down, shaken together, and running over. If it is to benefit you alone, the circle or circuit is not formed.

A successful person loves his work and expresses himself fully. True success is contingent upon a higher ideal than mere accumulation of riches. The person of success is one who possesses great psychological and spiritual understanding, and whose work benefits others.

CHAPTER EIGHT

The Inventiveness of Your Subconscious Mind

Nikola Tesla was a brilliant electrical scientist who brought forth amazing inventions in the late-nineteenth and early twentieth centuries. When an idea for a new invention entered Tesla's mind, he would build it up in his imagination, knowing that his subconscious would construct and reveal to his conscious mind all the parts needed for its manufacture. Through quietly contemplating every possible improvement, he spent no time in correcting defects, and was able to give technicians perfect plans for the product.

"Invariably," he said, "my device works as I imagined it should. In twenty years there has not been a single exception."

When you have what you term "a difficult decision" to make, or when you fail to see the solution to a problem, begin at once to think constructively about it. If you are fearful and worried, you are not really thinking. True thinking is free from fear.

Here is a simple technique to receive inner guidance on any subject: Quiet the mind and still the body. Go to a quiet place where you won't be disturbed—preferably lying on a bed, sofa, or in a recliner. Mobilize your attention; focus your thoughts on the solution to the problem. Try to solve it with your conscious mind. Think how happy you would be with the perfect solution. Sense the feeling you would have if the right answer were yours now. Let your mind play with this mood in a relaxed way; then drop off to sleep. When you awaken, and do not have the answer, get busy about something else. When you are preoccupied with something else, the answer will probably come into your mind like toast pops from out of a toaster.

The secret of guidance or right action is to mentally devote yourself to the right answer, until you find its response in you. The response is a feeling, an inner awareness, and an overpowering hunch whereby *you know that you know*. In such cases, you have used the infinite power of your subconscious to the point where *it begins to use you*. You cannot fail or make a false step while operating under the subconscious wisdom within you.

CHAPTER NINE

Your Subconscious Mind and Marital Problems

Recently a young couple, married for only a few months, was seeking a divorce. I discovered that the young man had a constant fear that his wife would leave him. He expected rejection, and he believed that she would be unfaithful. These thoughts haunted him and became an obsession. His mental attitude was one of separation and suspicion. His own feeling of loss and separation operated through the relationship. This brought about a condition in accordance with the mental pattern behind it.

His wife left home and asked for a divorce, which is what he feared and believed would happen.

Divorce occurs first in the mind; the legal proceedings follow. These two young people were full of resentment, fear, suspicion, and anger. These attitudes weaken and debilitate the whole being. The couple began to realize what they had been doing with their minds. These two people returned together at my suggestion and experimented with *prayer therapy*, a method we will learn.

Each one practiced radiating to the other love, peace, harmony, health, and good will. They alternated in reading the Psalms every night. Their marriage began growing more beautiful every day.

Now, divorce is an individual problem. It cannot be generalized. In some cases, no marriage should have occurred to begin with. In other cases, divorce is not the solution. Divorce may be right for one person and wrong for another. A divorced woman may be far more sincere and noble than many of her married sisters, who are perhaps living a lie.

For couples that wish to *stay together* the solution is to *pray together*. Here is a three-step program in prayer therapy.

FIRST

Never carry over from one day to another accumulated irritations arising from little disappointments. Forgive each other for any sharpness before you retire at night. The moment you awaken, claim infinite intelligence is guiding you in all ways. Send out thoughts of peace, harmony, and love to your partner, to all family members, and to the entire world.

SECOND
Say grace at breakfast. Give thanks for the wonderful food, for your abundance, and for all your blessings. Make sure that no problems, worries, or arguments enter into the table conversation; the same applies at dinnertime. Say to your partner, "I appreciate all you are doing, and I radiate love and good will to you all day long."

THIRD
Spouses should alternate in praying each night. Do not take your marriage partner for granted. Show your appreciation and love. Think appreciation and good will, rather than condemnation, criticism, and nagging. Before going to sleep read the 23rd, 27th, and 91st Psalms; the 11th chapter of Hebrews; the 13th chapter of I Corinthians; and other great texts of the Bible.

As you practice these steps, your marriage will grow more blessed through the years.

CHAPTER TEN

Your Subconscious Mind and Happiness

There is a phrase in the Bible: *Choose ye this day whom ye will serve.*

You have the freedom to *choose happiness.* This may seem extraordinarily simple—and it is. Perhaps this is why so many people stumble over the way to happiness; they do not see the simplicity of the key to happiness. The great things of life are simple, dynamic, and creative.

St. Paul reveals how you can think your way into a life of dynamic power and happiness in these words: *Finally, brethren, whatsoever things are true, whatsoever things are honest, whatsoever things are just, whatsoever things are pure, whatsoever things are lovely, whatsoever things are of good report; if there be any virtue, and if there be any praise, think on these things.* (Philippians 4:8)

There is one very important point about being happy. You must sincerely *desire* to be happy. Some people have been depressed, dejected, and unhappy for so long that when they are suddenly made happy by some joyous news they actually feel uncomfortable. They have become so accustomed to the old mental patterns that they do not feel at home being happy. They long for the familiar depressed state.

Begin now to choose happiness. Here is how: When you open your eyes in the morning, say to yourself: *Divine order takes charge of my life today and every day. All things work together for good for me today. This is a new and wonderful day for me. There will never be another day like this one. I am divinely guided all day long, and whatever I do will prosper. Divine love surrounds me, enfolds me, and enwraps me, and I go forth in peace. Whenever my attention wanders away from what is good and constructive, I will immediately bring it back to the contemplation of that which is lovely and of good report. I am a spiritual and mental magnet attracting to myself all things that bless and prosper me. I am going to be a wonderful success in all my undertakings today. I am definitely going to be happy all day long.*

Start each day in this manner; you will then be choosing happiness.

CHAPTER ELEVEN

Your Subconscious Mind and Harmonious Relationships

atthew 7:12 says, *All things whatsoever ye would that men should do unto you, do ye even so to them.*

This passage has outer and inner meanings. We are interested in its inner meaning, which is: As you would that men should *think* about you, think about them. As you would that men should *feel* about you, feel about them. As you would want men to *act* toward you, act toward them.

For example, you may be polite and courteous to someone in your office, but inside you are critical and resentful. Such negative thoughts are highly destructive to you. You are actually taking mental poisons, which rob you of enthusiasm, strength, guidance, and good will. These negative thoughts and emotions sink into your subconscious, and cause you all kinds of difficulties and maladies.

Matthew 7:1-2 says, *Judge not, that ye not be judged. For with what judgment ye judge, ye shall be judged; and with what measure ye shall mete, it shall be measured to you again.*

The study and application of these verses, and their inner truth, provides the key to harmonious relations. To judge is to think, to reach a mental verdict or conclusion in your mind. Your thoughts are creative, therefore, you actually create in your own experience what you think and feel about another person. It is also true that the suggestion you give to another, you give to yourself.

Now, there *are* difficult people in the world who are twisted and distorted mentally. They are malconditioned. Many are mental delinquents, argumentative, uncooperative, cantankerous, and cynical. They are sick psychologically. Many people have deformed and distorted minds, probably warped during childhood. Many have congenital deformities. You would not condemn a person who had tuberculosis, nor should you condemn someone who is mentally ill. You should have compassion and understanding. *To understand all is to forgive all.*

At the same time, do not permit people to take advantage of you and gain their point by temper tantrums, crying jags, or so-called heart attacks. These people are dictators who try to enslave you and make you do their bidding. Be firm but kind, and refuse to yield. *Appeasement never wins.* You are here to fulfill your ideal and to remain true to the eternal verities and spiritual values of life.

Give no one the power to deflect you from your goal, your aim in life, which is to express your hidden talents to the world, to serve humanity, and to reveal more and more of God's wisdom, truth, and beauty. Know definitely that whatever contributes to your peace, happiness, and fulfillment must, of necessity, bless all who walk the earth. The harmony of the part is the harmony of the whole, for the whole is in the part, and the part in the whole.

CHAPTER TWELVE

How Your Subconscious Mind Removes Mental Blocks

A young man asked Socrates how he could get wisdom. Socrates replied, "Come with me." He took the lad to a river, pushed the boy's head under the water, held it there until the boy was gasping for air, then relaxed and released his head. When the boy regained his composure, the teacher asked, "What did you desire most when you were under water?"

"I wanted air," said the boy.

Socrates told him, "When you want wisdom as much as you wanted air, you will receive it."

Likewise, when you possess an intense desire to overcome any block or addiction, and you reach a clear-cut decision that there is a way out, and that is the course you wish to follow, then victory and triumph are assured.

If you are an alcoholic or drug addict, begin by admitting it. Do not dodge the issue. Many people remain alcoholics because they refuse to admit it. If you have a burning desire to free yourself from any destructive habit, you are fifty-one percent healed. When you have a greater desire to give up a habit than to continue it, you will gain complete freedom.

Whatever thought you anchor the mind upon, the mind magnifies. If you engage the mind on the concept of freedom from habit and peace of mind, you generate feelings that gradually emotionalize the concept of freedom and peace. Whatever idea you emotionalize is accepted by your subconscious and brought to pass.

Use these steps to help cope with addiction:

FIRST
Get still; quiet the wheels of the mind. Enter into a sleepy, drowsy state. In this relaxed, peaceful, receptive state you are preparing for the second step.

SECOND
Take a brief phrase, which can readily be graven on the memory, and repeat it over and over as a lullaby. Use the phrase: *Sobriety and peace of mind are mine now, and I give thanks.* To prevent the mind from wandering, repeat the phrase aloud or sketch its pronunciation with

your lips and tongue as you say it mentally. This helps its entry into your subconscious. Do this for five minutes or more. You will find a deep emotional response.

THIRD

Just before going to sleep, imagine a friend or loved one in front of you. Your eyes closed, you are relaxed and at peace. The loved one or friend is subjectively present, and is saying to you, "Congratulations!" You see the smile; you hear the voice. You mentally touch the hand; it is all vivid and real. The word "congratulations" implies *complete freedom*. Hear it over and over until you get the subconscious reaction that satisfies.

CHAPTER THIRTEEN

How to Stay
Young in Spirit Forever

Your subconscious never grows old. It is part of the universal mind of God, which was never born and will never die.

Patience, kindness, veracity, humility, good will, harmony, and brotherly love are eternal attributes, which never age. If you continue to generate these qualities, you will remain young in spirit.

During my many years of public life, I have studied the careers of famous people who have continued their productivity well beyond the normal span of life. Some achieved their greatness in old age. I have also met and known countless individuals of no prominence who, in their lesser sphere, belong to those hardy mortals who have proven that old age of itself does not destroy the creative powers of the mind and body.

My father learned French at sixty-five, and became an authority on it at seventy. He made a study of Gaelic when he was over sixty, and became a well-regarded teacher of the subject. He assisted my sister in a school of higher learning and continued to do so until he passed away at ninety-nine. His mind was as clear at ninety-nine as it was at twenty. Moreover, his handwriting and reasoning powers improved with age.

A Hollywood screenwriter told me that he had to write scripts that would cater to the twelve-year-old mind. This is a tragic state of affairs if the great masses of people are expected to be emotionally and spiritually mature. It means the emphasis is placed on youth in spite of how youth stands for inexperience, lack of discernment, and hasty judgment.

Old age really means the contemplation of the truths of God from the highest standpoint. Realize that you are on an endless journey, a series of important steps in the ceaseless, tireless, endless ocean of life. Then, with the Psalmist, you will say, *They shall still bring forth fruit in old age; they shall be fat and flourishing.* (Psalm 92:14)

You are a child of Infinite Life, which knows no end, a child of Eternity.

JOSEPH MURPHY was born in 1898 on the southern coast of Ireland. Raised in a devout Catholic family, Murphy had planned on joining the priesthood. As young man he instead relocated to America to make his career as a chemist and druggist. After running a pharmacy counter at New York's Algonquin Hotel, Murphy began studying mystical and metaphysical ideas. In the 1940s he became a popular New Thought minister and writer. Murphy wrote prolifically on the autosuggestive and mystical faculties of the human mind. He became widely known for his metaphysical classic, *The Power of Your Subconscious Mind*, which has sold millions of copies since it first appeared in 1963. Considered one of the pioneering voices of New Thought and affirmative-thinking philosophy, Murphy died in Laguna Hills, California, in 1981.

MITCH HOROWITZ, who abridged and introduced this volume, is the PEN Award-winning author of books including *Occult America* and *The Miracle Club: How Thoughts Become Reality*. *The Washington Post* says Mitch "treats esoteric ideas and movements with an even-handed intellectual studiousness that is too often lost in today's raised-voice discussions." Follow him @MitchHorowitz.

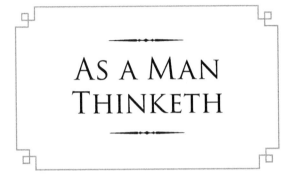

AS A MAN
THINKETH

As a Man Thinketh

by James Allen

*The Extraordinary Classic on Remaking
Your Life Through Your Thoughts*

Abridged and Introduced
by Mitch Horowitz

THE CONDENSED CLASSICS LIBRARY™

Contents

INTRODUCTION
Why James Allen Still Matters
by Mitch Horowitz 57

FOREWORD 67

CHAPTER ONE
Thought and Character 69

CHAPTER TWO
Effect of Thought on Circumstances 73

CHAPTER THREE
Thought and Purpose 83

CHAPTER FOUR
The Thought-Factor in Achievement 87

CHAPTER FIVE
Visions and Ideals 93

CHAPTER SIX
Serenity 97

ABOUT THE AUTHORS 100

Why James Allen Still Matters
By Mitch Horowitz

James Allen's literary career was short, ranging
roughly from the publication of his first book in
1901 to his death in 1912. Yet these few years of
output resulted in nearly twenty books, including
one of the most widely read inspirational works of our
time: *As a Man Thinketh.*

Allen's book became read in households where
few or no other positive-mind books were found. His
methods of mental creativity and ethical self-seeking set
the template for much of the metaphysical culture in
America in the twentieth century. In a sense, the key to
understanding Allen's work appears in the details of his
own life. The writer's journey from "poverty to power,"
to use his phrase, was Allen's greatest creation.

*   *   *

James Allen was born in 1864 in Leicester, an industrial town in central England. His father, William,
was a successful knitting manufacturer who cultivated
James's taste in books and philosophy. A downturn in
the textile trade drove William out of business, and
in 1879 he traveled to New York City to look for new
work. His plan was to get settled and pay for the rest of
the family to join him. But the unthinkable occurred.
On the brink of the Christmas season, just after James
had turned 15, word came back to the Allen household
that the family patriarch was dead. William had been
found robbed and murdered two days after reaching
New York. His battered body, with pockets emptied,
lay in a city hospital.

James's mother, Martha, a woman who could not
read or write, found herself in charge of James and
his two younger brothers, with no means of support.
"Young Jim" would have to leave school and find work
as a factory knitter. The teenager had been his father's
favorite. An avid reader, James had spent hours ques-
tioning him about life, death, religion, politics, and
Shakespeare. "My boy," William told him, "I'll make a
scholar of you." Those hopes were gone.

James took up employment locally as a framework
knitter, a job that occupied his energies for the next
nine years. He sometimes worked fifteen-hour days.

But even amid the strains of factory life, he retained the refined, studious bearing that his father had cultivated. When his workmates went out drinking, or caught up on sleep, Allen studied and read two to three hours a day. Coworkers called him "the Saint" and "the Parson."

Allen read through his father's collected works of Shakespeare, as well as books of ethics and religion. He grew determined to discover the "central purpose" of life. At age twenty-four, he found the book that finally seemed to reveal it to him: *The Light of Asia* by Edwin Arnold. The epic poem introduced Allen, along with a generation of Victorians, to the ideas of Buddhism. Under its influence, Allen came to believe that the true aim of all religion is self-development and inner refinement.

Shortly after discovering *The Light of Asia*, Allen experienced a turning point in his outer life, as well. Around 1889 he found new employment in London as a private secretary and stationer—markedly friendlier vocations to the bookish man than factory work. In London he also met his wife and intellectual partner, Lily.

By the mid-1890s, Allen had deepened his inquiry into spiritual philosophies, immersing himself in the works of John Milton, Ralph Waldo Emerson, Walt

Whitman, and early translations of the *Bhagavad Gita*, *Tao Te Ching*, and the sayings of Buddha.

He marveled over the commonalities in the world's religions. "The man who says, 'My religion is true, and my neighbor's is false,' has not yet discovered the truth in his own religion," he wrote, "for when a man has done that, he will see the Truth in all religions."

Allen also grew interested in the ideas of America's New Thought culture through the work of Ralph Waldo Trine, Orison Swett Marden, and, later, Christian D. Larson. His reading of New Thought, or positive-mind, literature sharpened his spiritual outlook—in particular his idea that our thoughts are causative and determine our destiny.

By 1898, Allen found an outlet for his intellectual interests. He began writing for the *Herald of the Golden Age*. In addition to metaphysical topics, the journal was an early voice for vegetarianism and humane treatment of animals, ideas that Allen had discovered in Buddhism. In 1901, he published his first book of practical philosophy, *From Poverty to Power*. The work extolled the creative agencies of the mind, placing equal emphasis on Christian ethics and New Thought metaphysics. The following year, Allen launched his own mystical magazine, the *Light of Reason*, and soon came another book, *All These Things Added*.

It was a period of tremendous productivity, capped in 1903 by Allen's third and most influential work—the short, immensely powerful meditation, *As a Man Thinketh*, which you are about to experience. The title is loosely adapted from a caution against hypocrisy in Proverbs 23:7: "As he thinketh in his heart, so is he." In Allen's eyes, that brief statement captured his core philosophy—that a man's thought, if not the cause of his circumstances, is the cause of *himself,* and shapes the tenor of his life.

The phrase "as a man thinketh" became the informal motto of the New Thought movement, adopted and repeated by motivational writers throughout the century. Allen's book is marked by memorable, aphoristic lessons, which have withstood the passage of time. *As a Man Thinketh* defines achievement in deeply personal terms: "You will become as small as your controlling desire; as great as your dominant aspiration."

Toward the end of *As a Man Thinketh*, Allen writes in a manner that amounts to autobiography:

> *Here is a youth hard pressed by poverty and labor; confined long hours in an unhealthy workshop; unschooled, and lacking all the arts of refinement. But he dreams of better things: he*

*thinks of intelligence, of refinement, of grace and
beauty. He conceives of, mentally builds up, an
ideal condition of life; vision of a wider liberty
and a larger scope takes possession of him; unrest
urges him to action, and he utilizes all his spare
time and means, small though they are, to the
development of his latent powers and resources.
Very soon so altered has his mind become that the
workshop can no longer hold him.*

As a personal rule, Allen always used his life experiences as the backbone of his teaching. "He never wrote
theories," Lily noted in 1913, "or for the sake of writing;
but he wrote when he had a message, and it became a
message *only when he had lived it out in his own life*, and
knew that it was good."

The impact of *As a Man Thinketh* was not fully
felt during Allen's lifetime, but the book brought him
enough of an audience (and sufficient pay) so that he
was able to quit secretarial work and commit himself to
writing and editing fulltime. On its publication, Allen,
Lily, and their daughter, Nora, moved to the southern
English costal town of Ilfracombe, where he spent the
remainder of his life. He wrote books at a remarkable
pace, often more than one a year, producing nineteen
works. Allen's days assumed a meticulous routine of

meditating, writing, walking in nature, and gardening. He work habits never flagged. "Thoroughness is genius," he wrote in 1904.

For all of his creative output, Allen struggled with fragile health. Lily wrote of her husband faltering from an illness in late 1911. On January 24, 1912, Allen died at home in Ilfracombe at age 47, probably of tuberculosis.

In an obituary of January 27, the *Ilfracombe Chronicle* noted: "Mr. Allen's books . . . are perhaps better known abroad, especially in America, than in England." Indeed, the twentieth century's leading American writers of motivational thought—from Napoleon Hill to Norman Vincent Peale—read and noted the influence of *As a Man Thinketh*. Dale Carnegie said the book had "a lasting and profound effect on my life." The cofounder of Alcoholics Anonymous, Bob Smith, called it a favorite. The black-nationalist pioneer Marcus Garvey embraced the book's do-for-self ethic and adapted the slogan "As Man Thinks So Is He" on the cover of his newspaper, *Blackman*. In years ahead, the book's influence showed up in myriad places: An adolescent Michael Jackson told a friend that it was his "favorite book in the world;" NFL Hall of Famer Curtis Martin credited *As a Man Thinketh* with helping him overcome pain and injury; businessman and Oprah Winfrey partner

Stedman Graham said Allen's work helped him attain "real freedom."

Yet the full impact of *As a Man Thinketh* can best be seen in the successive generations of everyday readers who embraced its aphoristic lessons in directing one's thoughts to higher aims, and to understanding success as the outer manifestation of inner development.

"Men do not attract that which they *want*," Allen told readers, "but that which they *are*." In that sense, Allen attracted a vast following of people who mirrored the ordinary circumstances from which he arose—and whose hopes for a better, nobler existence were reflected back to them in the example of his life.

This gentle abridgement of *As a Man Thinketh* is intended to make the work and its message available to you in a single sitting. I have based it upon the earliest American edition of *As a Man Thinketh*, published in Chicago in 1905, and it contains the full nature of Allen's message. My one significant excision has been his short chapter on health, in which I think the author drew too complete and hasty a confluence, at least in my mind as an observer and lover of New Thought, between thoughts and disease. With this excision, I believe the book functions better as a moral philosophy, and it is possible that in hindsight, the author, himself a publisher and editor, would have agreed.

What you are about to experience is a philosophy of spiritual and mental governance of character and circumstance, which may prove as life-altering to you as it has to countless devotees of this powerful meditation for more than a century.

> *Mind is the Master power that moulds and makes, And Man is Mind, and evermore he takes The tool of Thought, and, shaping what he wills, Brings forth a thousand joys, a thousand ills:— He thinks in secret, and it comes to pass: Environment is but his looking-glass.*

FOREWORD

This little volume (the result of meditation and experience) is not intended as an exhaustive treatise on the much-written-upon subject of the power of thought. It is suggestive rather than explanatory, its object being to stimulate men and women to the discovery and perception of the truth that—

"They themselves are makers of themselves"

by virtue of the thoughts which they choose and encourage; that mind is the master-weaver, both of the inner garment of character and the outer garment of circumstance, and that, as they may have hitherto woven in ignorance and pain they may now weave in enlightenment and happiness.

—James Allen

Chapter One

Thought and Character

The aphorism, "As a man thinketh in his heart so is he," not only embraces the whole of a man's being, but is so comprehensive as to reach out to every condition and circumstance of his life. A man is literally *what he thinks,* his character being the complete sum of all his thoughts.

As the plant springs from, and could not be without the seed, so every act of a man springs from the hidden seeds of thought, and could not have appeared without them. This applies equally to those acts called "spontaneous" and "unpremeditated," as to those that are deliberately executed.

Act is the blossom of thought, and joy and suffering are its fruits; thus does a man garner in the sweet and bitter fruitage of his own husbandry.

Man is a growth by law, and not a creation by artifice, and cause and effect is as absolute and undeviating in the hidden realm of thought as in the world of visible and material things. A noble and Godlike character is not a thing of favor or chance, but is the natural result of continued effort in right thinking, the effect of long-cherished association with Godlike thoughts. An ignoble and bestial character, by the same process, is the result of the continued harboring of groveling thoughts.

Man is made or unmade by himself; in the armory of thought he forges the weapons by which he destroys himself; he also fashions the tools with which he builds for himself heavenly mansions of joy and strength and peace. By the right choice and true application of thought, man ascends to the Divine Perfection; by the abuse and wrong application of thought, he descends below the level of the beast. Between these two extremes are all the grades of character, and man is their maker and master.

Of all the beautiful truths pertaining to the soul which have been restored and brought to light in this age, none is more gladdening or fruitful of divine promise and confidence than this—that man is the master of thought, the moulder of character, and the maker and shaper of condition, environment, and destiny.

As a being of Power, Intelligence, and Love, and the lord of his own thoughts, man holds the key to every situation, and contains within himself that transforming and regenerative agency by which he may make himself what he wills.

Man is always the master, even in his weaker and most abandoned state; but in his weakness and degradation he is the foolish master who misgoverns his "household." When he begins to reflect upon his condition, and to search diligently for the Law upon which his being is established, he then becomes the wise master, directing his energies with intelligence, and fashioning his thoughts to fruitful issues. Such is the *conscious* master, and man can only thus become by discovering *within himself* the laws of thought; which discovery is totally a matter of application, self analysis, and experience.

Only by much searching and mining, are gold and diamonds obtained, and man can find every truth connected with his being, if he will dig deep into the mine of his soul; and that he is the maker of his character, the moulder of his life, and the builder of his destiny, he may unerringly prove, if he will watch, control, and alter his thoughts, tracing their effects upon himself, upon others, and upon his life and circumstances, linking cause and effect by patient practice and investigation, and utilizing his every experience, even to the most trivial, everyday occurrence, as a means of obtaining that knowledge of himself which is Understanding,

Wisdom, Power. In this direction, as in no other, is the law absolute that "He that seeketh findeth; and to him that knocketh it shall be opened;" for only by patience, practice, and ceaseless importunity can a man enter the Door of the Temple of Knowledge.

Chapter Two

Effect of Thought
on Circumstances

A man's mind may be likened to a garden, which may be intelligently cultivated or allowed to run wild; but whether cultivated or neglected, it must, and will, *bring forth*. If no useful seeds are *put* into it, then an abundance of useless weed-seeds will *fall* therein, and will continue to produce their kind.

Just as a gardener cultivates his plot, keeping it free from weeds, and growing the flowers and fruits which he requires, so may a man tend the garden of his mind, weeding out all the wrong, useless, and impure thoughts, and cultivating toward perfection the flowers and fruits of right, useful, and pure thoughts. By pursuing this process, a man sooner or later discovers that he is the master-gardener of his soul, the director of his life. He also reveals, within himself, the laws of thought, and understands, with ever-increasing accuracy, how the thought-forces and mind elements operate in the shaping of his character, circumstances, and destiny.

Thought and character are one, and as character can only manifest and discover itself through environment and circumstance, the outer conditions of a person's life will always be found to be harmoniously related to his inner state. This does not mean that a man's circumstances at any given time are an indication of his *entire* character, but that those circumstances are so intimately connected with some vital thought-element within himself that, for the time being, they are indispensable to his development.

Every man is where he is by the law of his being; the thoughts which he has built into his character have brought him there, and in the arrangement of his life there is no element of chance, but all is the result of a law which cannot err. This is just as true of those who feel "out of harmony" with their surroundings as of those who are contented with them.

As a progressive and evolving being, man is where he is that he may learn that he may grow; and as he learns the spiritual lesson that any circumstance contains for him, it passes away and gives place to other circumstances.

Man is buffeted by circumstances so long as he believes himself to be the creature of outside conditions, but when he realizes that he is a creative power, and that he may command the hidden soil and seeds of his being out of which circumstances grow, he then becomes the rightful master of himself.

The soul attracts that which it secretly harbors; that which it loves, and also that which it fears; it reaches the height of its cherished aspirations; it falls to the level of its unchastened desires—and circumstances are the means by which the soul receives its own.

Every thought-seed sown or allowed to fall into the mind, and to take root there, produces its own, blossoming sooner or later into act, and bearing its own fruitage of opportunity and circumstance. Good thoughts bear good fruit, bad thoughts bad fruit.

The outer world of circumstance shapes itself to the inner world of thought, and both pleasant and unpleasant external conditions are factors, which make for the ultimate good of the individual. As the reaper of his own harvest, man learns both by suffering and bliss.

Following the inmost desires, aspirations, thoughts, by which he allows himself to be dominated, a man at last arrives at their fruition and fulfillment in the outer conditions of his life. The laws of growth and adjustment everywhere obtain.

Circumstance does not make the man; it reveals him to himself. No such conditions can exist as descending into vice and its attendant sufferings apart from vicious inclinations, or ascending into virtue and its pure happiness without the continued cultivation of virtuous aspirations; and man, therefore, as the lord and master of thought, is the maker of himself, the shaper and author of environment. Even at birth the soul comes to its own, and through every step of its earthly pilgrimage it attracts those combinations of conditions which reveal itself, which are the reflections of its own purity and impurity, its strength and weakness.

Men do not attract that which they *want*, but that which they *are*. Their whims, fancies, and ambitions are thwarted at every step, but their inmost thoughts and desires are fed with their own food, be it foul or clean. The "divinity that shapes our ends" is in ourselves; it is our very self. Man is manacled only by himself: thought and action are the jailers of Fate—they imprison, being base; they are also the angels of Freedom—they liberate, being noble. Not what he wishes and prays for does a man get, but what he justly earns. His wishes and prayers are only gratified and answered when they harmonize with his thoughts and actions.

In the light of this truth, what, then, is the meaning of "fighting against circumstances?" It means that a man is continually revolting against an *effect* without, while all the time he is nourishing and preserving its *cause* in his heart. That cause may take the form of a conscious vice or an unconscious weakness; but whatever it is, it stubbornly retards the efforts of its possessor, and thus calls aloud for remedy.

Men are anxious to improve their circumstances, but are unwilling to improve themselves; they therefore remain bound. The man who does not shrink from self-crucifixion can never fail to accomplish the object upon which his heart is set. This is as true of earthly as of heavenly things. Even the man whose sole object is to acquire wealth must be prepared to make great personal sacrifices before he can accomplish his object; and how much more so he who would realize a strong and well-poised life?

Here is a man who is wretchedly poor. He is extremely anxious that his surroundings and home comforts should be improved, yet all the time he shirks his work, and considers he is justified in trying to deceive his employer on the ground of the insufficiency of his wages. Such a man does not understand the simplest rudiments of those principles which are the basis of true prosperity, and is not only totally unfitted to rise out of his wretchedness, but is actually attracting to himself a still deeper wretchedness by dwelling in, and acting out, indolent, deceptive, and unmanly thoughts.

Here is a rich man who is the victim of a painful and persistent disease as the result of gluttony. He is willing to give large sums of money to get rid of it, but he will not sacrifice his gluttonous desires. He wants to gratify his taste for rich and unnatural viands and have his health as well. Such a man is totally unfit to have health, because he has not yet learned the first principles of a healthy life.

Here is an employer of labor who adopts crooked measures to avoid paying the regulation wage, and, in the hope of making larger profits, reduces the wages of his work-people. Such a man is altogether unfitted for prosperity, and when he finds himself bankrupt, both as regards reputation and riches, he blames circumstances, not knowing that he is the sole author of his condition.

I have introduced these three cases merely as illustrative of the truth that man is the causer (though nearly always unconsciously) of his circumstances, and that, whilst aiming at a good end, he is continually frustrating its accomplishment by encouraging thoughts and desires which cannot possibly harmonize with that end. Such cases could be multiplied and varied almost indefinitely, but this is not necessary, as the reader can, if he so resolves, trace the action of the laws of thought in his own mind and life, and until this is done, mere external facts cannot serve as a ground of reasoning.

Circumstances, however, are so complicated, thought is so deeply rooted, and the conditions of happiness vary so vastly with individuals, that a man's entire soul-condition (although it may be known to himself) cannot be judged by another from the external aspect of his life alone. A man may be honest in certain directions, yet suffer privations; a man may be dishonest in certain directions, yet acquire wealth; but the conclusion usually formed that the one man fails *because of his particular honesty,* and that the other prospers *because of his particular dishonesty,* is the result of a superficial judgment, which assumes that the dishonest man is almost totally corrupt, and the honest man almost entirely virtuous. In the light of a deeper knowledge and wider experience, such judgment is found to be erroneous. The dishonest man may have some admirable virtues, which the other does not possess; and the honest man obnoxious vices which are absent in the other. The honest man reaps the good results of his honest thoughts and acts; he also brings upon himself the sufferings which his vices produce. The dishonest man likewise garners his own suffering and happiness.

Good thoughts and actions can never produce bad results; bad thoughts and actions can never produce good results. This is but saying that nothing can come from corn but corn, nothing from nettles but nettles. Men understand this law in the natural world, and work with it; but few understand it in the mental and moral world (though its operation there is just as simple and undeviating), and they, therefore, do not cooperate with it.

Suffering is *always* the effect of wrong thought in some direction. It is an indication that the individual is out of harmony with himself, with the Law of his being. The sole and supreme use of suffering is to purify, to burn out all that is useless and impure. Suffering ceases for him who is pure. There could be no object in burning gold after the dross had been removed, and a perfectly pure and enlightened being could not suffer.

The circumstances that a man encounters with suffering are the result of his own mental inharmony. The circumstances that a man encounters with blessedness are the result of his own mental harmony. Blessedness, not material possessions, is the measure of right thought; wretchedness, not lack of material possessions, is the measure of wrong thought. A man may be cursed and rich; he may be blessed and poor. Blessedness and riches are only joined together when the riches are rightly and wisely used; and the poor man only descends into wretchedness when he regards his lot as a burden unjustly imposed.

Indigence and indulgence are the two extremes of wretchedness. They are both equally unnatural and the result of mental disorder. A man is not rightly conditioned until he is a happy, healthy, and prosperous being; and happiness, health, and prosperity are the result of a harmonious adjustment of the inner with the outer, of the man with his surroundings.

A man only begins to be a man when he ceases to whine and revile, and commences to search for the hidden justice that regulates his life. And as he adapts his mind to that regulating factor, he ceases to accuse others as the cause of his condition, and builds himself up in strong and noble thoughts; ceases to kick against circumstances, but begins to *use* them as aids to his more rapid progress, and as a means of discovering the hidden powers and possibilities within himself.

Law, not confusion, is the dominating principle in the universe; justice, not injustice, is the soul and substance of life; and righteousness, not corruption, is the moulding and moving force in the spiritual government of the world. This being so, man has but to right himself to find that the universe is right; and during the process of putting himself right he will find that as he alters his thoughts towards things and other people, things and other people will alter towards him.

Let a man radically alter his thoughts, and he will be astonished at the rapid transformation it will effect in the material conditions of his life. Men imagine that thought can be kept secret, but it cannot; it rapidly crystallizes into habit, and habit solidifies into circumstance. A particular train of thought persisted in, be it good or bad, cannot fail to produce its results on the character and circumstances. A man cannot *directly* choose his circumstances, but he can choose his thoughts, and so indirectly, yet surely, shape his circumstances.

Nature helps every man to the gratification of the thoughts which he most encourages, and opportunities are presented which will most speedily bring to the surface both the good and evil thoughts.

Let a man cease from his sinful thoughts, and all the world will soften towards him, and be ready to help him; let him put away his weakly and sickly thoughts, and lo! opportunities will spring up on every hand to aid his strong resolves; let him encourage good thoughts, and no hard fate shall bind him down to wretchedness and shame. The world is your kaleidoscope, and the varying combinations of colors, which at every succeeding moment it presents to you, are the exquisitely adjusted pictures of your ever-moving thoughts.

CHAPTER THREE

Thought and Purpose

Until thought is linked with purpose there is no intelligent accomplishment. With the majority the bark of thought is allowed to "drift" upon the ocean of life. Aimlessness is a vice, and such drifting must not continue for him who would steer clear of catastrophe and destruction.

They who have no central purpose in their life fall an easy prey to petty worries, fears, troubles, and self-pityings, all of which are indications of weakness, which lead, just as surely as deliberately planned sins (though by a different route) to failure, unhappiness, and loss, for weakness cannot persist in a power-evolving universe.

A man should conceive of a legitimate purpose in his heart, and set out to accomplish it. He should make this purpose the centralizing point of his thoughts. It may take the form of a spiritual ideal, or it may be a worldly object, according to his nature at the time being; but whichever it is, he should steadily focus his thought-forces upon the object which he has set before him. He should make this purpose his supreme duty, and should devote himself to its attainment, not allowing his thoughts to wander away into ephemeral fancies, longings, and imaginings. This is the royal road to self-control and true concentration of thought. Even if he fails again and again to accomplish his purpose (as he necessarily must until weakness is overcome), the *strength of character gained* will be the measure of his *true* success, and this will form a new starting-point for future power and triumph.

Those who are not prepared for the apprehension of a *great* purpose should fix the thoughts upon the faultless performance of their duty, no matter how insignificant their task may appear. Only in this way can the thoughts be gathered and focused, and resolution and energy be developed, which being done, there is nothing which may not be accomplished.

The weakest soul, knowing its own weakness, and believing this truth—*that strength can only be developed by effort and practice,* will, thus believing, at once begin to exert itself, and, adding effort to effort, patience to patience, and strength to strength, will never cease to develop, and will at last grow divinely strong.

As the physically weak man can make himself strong by careful and patient training, so the man of weak thoughts can make them strong by exercising himself in right thinking.

To put away aimlessness and weakness, and to begin to think with purpose, is to enter the ranks of those strong ones who only recognize failure as one of the pathways to attainment; who make all conditions serve them, and who think strongly, attempt fearlessly, and accomplish masterfully.

Having conceived of his purpose, a man should mentally mark out a *straight* pathway to its achievement, looking neither to the right nor the left. Doubts and fears should be rigorously excluded; they are disintegrating elements, which break up the straight line of effort, rendering it crooked, ineffectual, useless. Thoughts of doubt and fear never accomplished anything, and never can. They always lead to failure. Purpose, energy, power to do, and all strong thoughts cease when doubt and fear creep in.

The will to do springs from the knowledge that we *can* do. Doubt and fear are the great enemies of knowledge, and he who encourages them, who does not slay them, thwarts himself at every step.

He who has conquered doubt and fear has conquered failure. His every thought is allied with power, and all difficulties are bravely met and wisely overcome. His purposes are seasonably planted, and they bloom and bring forth fruit, which does not fall prematurely to the ground.

Thought allied fearlessly to purpose becomes creative force: he who *knows* this is ready to become something higher and stronger than a mere bundle of wavering thoughts and fluctuating sensations; he who *does* this has become the conscious and intelligent wielder of his mental powers.

CHAPTER FOUR

The Thought-Factor
in Achievement

All that a man achieves and all that he fails to achieve is the direct result of his own thoughts. In a justly ordered universe, where loss of equipoise would mean total destruction, individual responsibility must be absolute. A man's weakness and strength, purity and impurity, are his own, and not another man's; they are brought about by himself, and not by another; and they can only be altered by himself, never by another. His condition is also his own, and not another man's. His suffering and his happiness are evolved from within. As he thinks, so he is; as he continues to think, so he remains.

A strong man cannot help a weaker unless that weaker is *willing* to be helped, and even then the weak man must become strong of himself; he must, by his own efforts, develop the strength which he admires in another. None but himself can alter his condition.

It has been usual for men to think and to say, "Many men are slaves because one is an oppressor; let us hate the oppressor." Now, however, there is amongst an increasing few a tendency to reverse this judgment, and to say, "One man is an oppressor because many are slaves; let us despise the slaves." The truth is that oppressor and slave are cooperators in ignorance, and, while seeming to afflict each other, are in reality afflicting themselves. A perfect Knowledge perceives the action of law in the weakness of the oppressed and the misapplied power of the oppressor; a perfect Love, seeing the suffering, which both states entail, condemns neither; a perfect Compassion embraces both oppressor and oppressed.

He who has conquered weakness, and has put away all selfish thoughts, belongs neither to oppressor nor oppressed. He is free.

A man can only rise, conquer, and achieve by lifting up his thoughts. He can only remain weak, and abject, and miserable by refusing to lift up his thoughts.

Before a man can achieve anything, even in worldly things, he must lift his thoughts above slavish animal indulgence. He may not, in order to succeed, give up *all* animality and selfishness, by any means; but a portion of it must, at least, be sacrificed. A man whose first thought is bestial indulgence could neither think clearly nor plan methodically; he could not find and develop his latent resources, and would fail in any undertaking. Not having commenced to manfully control his thoughts, he is not in a position to control affairs and to adopt serious responsibilities. He is not fit to act independently and stand alone. But he is limited only by the thoughts which he chooses.

There can be no progress, no achievement without sacrifice, and a man's worldly success will be in the measure that he sacrifices his confused animal thoughts, and fixes his mind on the development of his plans, and the strengthening of his resolution and self-reliance. And the higher he lifts his thoughts, the more manly, upright, and righteous he becomes, the greater will be his success, the more blessed and enduring will be his achievements.

The universe does not favor the greedy, the dishonest, the vicious, although on the mere surface it may sometimes appear to do so; it helps the honest, the magnanimous, the virtuous. All the great Teachers of the ages have declared this in varying forms, and to prove and know it a man has but to persist in making himself more and more virtuous by lifting up his thoughts.

Intellectual achievements are the result of thought consecrated to the search for knowledge, or for the beautiful and true in life and nature. Such achievements may be sometimes connected with vanity and ambition, but they are not the outcome of those characteristics; they are the natural outgrowth of long and arduous effort, and of pure and unselfish thoughts.

Spiritual achievements are the consummation of holy aspirations. He who lives constantly in the conception of noble and lofty thoughts, who dwells upon all that is pure and unselfish, will, as surely as the sun reaches its zenith and the moon its full, become wise and noble in character, and rise into a position of influence and blessedness.

Achievement, of whatever kind, is the crown of effort, the diadem of thought. By the aid of self-control, resolution, purity, righteousness, and well-directed thought a man ascends; by the aid of animality, indolence, impurity, corruption, and confusion of thought a man descends.

A man may rise to high success in the world, and even to lofty altitudes in the spiritual realm, and again descend into weakness and wretchedness by allowing arrogant, selfish, and corrupt thoughts to take possession of him.

Victories attained by right thought can only be maintained by watchfulness. Many give way when success is assured, and rapidly fall back into failure.

All achievements, whether in the business, intellectual, or spiritual world, are the result of definitely directed thought, are governed by the same law and are of the same method; the only difference lies in *the object of attainment.*

He who would accomplish little must sacrifice little; he who would achieve much must sacrifice much; he who would attain highly must sacrifice greatly.

CHAPTER FIVE

Visions and Ideals

The dreamers are the saviors of the world. As the visible world is sustained by the invisible, so men, through all their trials and sins and sordid vocations, are nourished by the beautiful visions of their solitary dreamers. Humanity cannot forget its dreamers; it cannot let their ideals fade and die; it lives in them; it knows them as the *realities* which it shall one day see and know.

Composer, sculptor, painter, poet, prophet, sage, these are the makers of the after-world, the architects of heaven. The world is beautiful because they have lived; without them, laboring humanity would perish.

He who cherishes a beautiful vision, a lofty ideal in his heart, will one day realize it. Cherish your visions; cherish your ideals; cherish the music that stirs in your heart, the beauty that forms in your mind, the loveliness that drapes your purest thoughts, for out of them will grow all delightful conditions, all heavenly environment; of these, if you but remain true to them, your world will at last be built.

To desire is to obtain; to aspire is to achieve. Shall man's basest desires receive the fullest measure of gratification, and his purest aspirations starve for lack of sustenance? Such is not the Law: such a condition of things can never obtain: "Ask and receive."

Dream lofty dreams, and as you dream, so shall you become. Your Vision is the promise of what you shall one day be; your Ideal is the prophecy of what you shall at last unveil.

The greatest achievement was at first and for a time a dream. The oak sleeps in the acorn; the bird waits in the egg; and in the highest vision of the soul a waking angel stirs. Dreams are the seedlings of realities.

Your circumstances may be uncongenial, but they shall not long remain so if you but perceive an Ideal and strive to reach it. You cannot travel *within* and stand still *without.* Here is a youth hard pressed by poverty and labor; confined long hours in an unhealthy workshop; unschooled, and lacking all the arts of refinement. But he dreams of better things; he thinks of intelligence, of refinement, of grace and beauty. He conceives of, mentally builds up, an ideal condition of life; the vision of a wider liberty and a larger scope takes possession of him;

unrest urges him to action, and he utilizes all his spare time and means, small though they are, to the development of his latent powers and resources. Very soon so altered has his mind become that the workshop can no longer hold him. It has become so out of harmony with his mentality that it falls out of his life as a garment is cast aside, and, with the growth of opportunities which fit the scope of his expanding powers, he passes out of it forever.

And you, too, will realize the Vision (not the idle wish) of your heart, be it base or beautiful, or a mixture of both, for you will always gravitate toward that which you, secretly, most love. Into your hands will be placed the exact results of your own thoughts; you will receive that which you earn; no more, no less. Whatever your present environment may be, you will fall, remain, or rise with your thoughts, your Vision, your Ideal. You will become as small as your controlling desire; as great as your dominant aspiration.

The thoughtless, the ignorant, and the indolent, seeing only the apparent effects of things and not the things themselves, talk of luck, of fortune, and chance. Seeing a man grow rich, they say, "How lucky he is!" Observing another become intellectual, they exclaim, "How highly favored he is!" And noting the saintly character and wide influence of another, they remark,

"How chance aids him at every turn!" They do not see the trials and failures and struggles which these men have voluntarily encountered in order to gain their experience; have no knowledge of the sacrifices they have made, of the undaunted efforts they have put forth, of the faith they have exercised, that they might overcome the apparently insurmountable, and realize the Vision of their heart. They do not know the darkness and the heartaches; they only see the light and joy, and call it "luck." They do not see the long and arduous journey, but only behold the pleasant goal, and call it "good fortune," do not understand the process, but only perceive the result, and call it "chance."

In all human affairs there are *efforts,* and there are *results,* and the strength of the effort is the measure of the result. Chance is not. "Gifts," powers, material, intellectual, and spiritual possessions are the fruits of effort; they are thoughts completed, objects accomplished, visions realized.

The Vision that you glorify in your mind, the Ideal that you enthrone in your heart—this you will build your life by, this you will become.

CHAPTER SIX

Serenity

Calmness of mind is one of the beautiful jewels of wisdom. It is the result of long and patient effort in self-control. Its presence is an indication of ripened experience, and of a more than ordinary knowledge of the laws and operations of thought.

A man becomes calm in the measure that he understands himself as a thought-evolved being, for such knowledge necessitates the understanding of others as the result of thought, and as he develops a right understanding, and sees more and more clearly the internal relations of things by the action of cause and effect, he ceases to fuss and fume and worry and grieve, and remains poised, steadfast, serene.

The calm man, having learned how to govern himself, knows how to adapt himself to others; and they, in turn, reverence his spiritual strength, and feel that they can learn of him and rely upon him. The more tranquil a man becomes, the greater is his success, his influence, his power for good. Even the ordinary trader will find his business prosperity increase as he develops a greater self-control and equanimity, for people will always prefer to deal with a man whose demeanor is strongly equable.

The strong, calm man is always loved and revered. He is like a shade-giving tree in a thirsty land, or a sheltering rock in a storm. "Who does not love a tranquil heart, a sweet-tempered, balanced life? It does not matter whether it rains or shines, or what changes come to those possessing these blessings, for they are always sweet, serene, and calm. That exquisite poise of character, which we call serenity, is the last lesson of culture; it is the flowering of life, the fruitage of the soul. It is precious as wisdom, more to be desired than gold—yea, than even fine gold. How insignificant mere money seeking looks in comparison with a serene life—a life that dwells in the ocean of Truth, beneath the waves, beyond the reach of tempests, in the Eternal Calm!

"How many people we know who sour their lives, who ruin all that is sweet and beautiful by explosive tempers, who destroy their poise of character, and make bad blood! It is a question whether the great majority of people do not ruin their lives and mar their happiness by lack of self-control. How few people we meet in life who are well balanced, who have that exquisite poise which is characteristic of the finished character!"

Yes, humanity surges with uncontrolled passion, is tumultuous with ungoverned grief, is blown about by anxiety and doubt. Only the wise man, only he whose thoughts are controlled and purified, makes the winds and the storms of the soul obey him.

Tempest-tossed souls, wherever ye may be, under whatsoever conditions ye may live, know this—in the ocean of life the isles of Blessedness are smiling, and the sunny shore of your ideal awaits your coming. Keep your hand firmly upon the helm of thought. In the bark of your soul reclines the commanding Master; He does but sleep: wake Him. Self-control is strength; Right Thought is mastery; Calmness is power. Say unto your heart, "Peace, be still!"

JAMES ALLEN was born in Leicester, in central England's industrial heartland, on November 28, 1864. He took his first job at age 15 to support his family after his father was murdered while looking for work in America in 1879. Allen worked as a factory knitter and later as a private secretary with various manufacturing companies. In 1901, he published his first book, *From Poverty to Power*. The following year, he left secretarial work to devote himself fulltime to writing, and in 1903 published his third and best-known work, *As a Man Thinketh*. At this time, Allen moved with his wife, Lily, and daughter, Nora, to Ilfracombe, England, where he continued to write books and articles, and, with Lily, to publish his spiritual journal, *The Light of Reason*, later retitled *The Epoch*. He died at age 47 on January 24, 1912, most likely of tuberculosis. Allen completed nineteen books during his career, several of which were published posthumously. *As a Man Thinketh* is considered one of the formative classics of modern inspirational thought.

MITCH HOROWITZ, who abridged and introduced this volume, is the PEN Award-winning author of books including *Occult America* and *The Miracle Club: How Thoughts Become Reality*. *The Washington Post* says Mitch "treats esoteric ideas and movements with an even-handed intellectual studiousness that is too often lost in today's raised-voice discussions." Follow him @MitchHorowitz.

THE
GAME OF LIFE
AND
HOW TO PLAY IT

The
Game of Life
and
How to Play it

by
Florence Scovel Shinn

The Timeless Classic on Successful Living

Abridged and Introduced
by Mitch Horowitz

THE CONDENSED CLASSICS LIBRARY™

CONTENTS

INTRODUCTION
Philosopher of Everyday Life 109

CHAPTER ONE
The Game 113

CHAPTER TWO
The Law of Prosperity 117

CHAPTER THREE
The Power of the Word 121

CHAPTER FOUR
The Law of Nonresistance 123

CHAPTER FIVE
The Law of Karma 125

CHAPTER SIX
**Casting the Burden
(Impressing the Subconscious)**................ 127

CHAPTER SEVEN
Love...133

CHAPTER EIGHT
Intuition or Guidance 137

CHAPTER NINE
**Perfect Self-Expression
or the Divine Design** 141

CHAPTER TEN
Denials and Affirmations...........................145

ABOUT THE AUTHORS 149

Philosopher of Everyday Life

Ask any fan of motivational or New Thought literature to name his or her favorite books, and chances are the list will include Florence Scovel Shinn's *The Game of Life and How to Play It.*

Shinn's book has been beloved among self-help readers since it first appeared in 1925. Yet it almost didn't appear at all. Shinn, a respected illustrator of children's literature, could not get New York publishers interested in her metaphysical philosophy. Finding no takers, the artist published the book herself.

Shinn's outlook is simple and decisive. Within you, she writes, exist three minds: the *conscious mind,* which you use to navigate daily life; the *subconscious mind,* which acts on suggestions, good or bad, from your conscious mind; and the *superconscious mind,* a spark of divine power within you. Your superconscious, she writes, possesses infinite awareness and the creative ability to remake your world. Shinn provides methods to get in tune with this higher mind, and thus "win" at the game of life.

What accounts for Shinn's longstanding popularity? Her ideas were not unique to her time. Contemporaneous metaphysical writers, such as William Walker Atkinson and Wallace D. Wattles, held similar views. Yet listening to Shinn always feels like hearing from a trusted friend—someone who understands our daily struggles and who doesn't talk above us; but who also isn't afraid to deliver tough advice and won't tolerate excuses. She insists that we get out there and test her methods on the field of life.

Shinn was a lasting influence on many leaders in the positive-thinking movement, including Emmett Fox, Norman Vincent Peale, and Louise Hay. It is notable that each of these figures is from a different generation: Fox, a popular New Thought minister, was a contemporary of Shinn's; Peale, a Methodist minister, rose to worldwide fame in the 1950s as the author of *The Power of Positive Thinking*; and Hay is widely known today as a pioneering New Age publisher and writer. Martin Luther King's eldest daughter, Yolanda, told me shortly before her death in 2007 that Shinn's writing had influenced her. This gives some sense of Shinn's range of impact.

While Shinn called life a "game," her own life was not easy—nor did she seek ease. Born Florence Scovel in Camden, New Jersey in 1871, she took a rare path as a female artist, attending the Pennsylvania Academy of Fine Arts. There she met her future husband, realist painter Everett Shinn. Married in 1898, they moved to New York's Greenwich Village, where they became part of the Ashcan School of American artists, a cohort known for depicting street scenes, tenements, and the immigrant experience. The couple divorced in 1912. While pursuing her own career as an illustrator, Shinn became a student of metaphysics, leading her to write *The Game of Life* and several other books. She also became a popular spiritual lecturer and counselor. She died in Manhattan in 1940.

One of the defining elements of Shinn's work is its bravery. Shinn neither sought, nor received, mainstream approval. Instead, she embodied a core ideal of American metaphysics: that the common person, the everyday man or woman, is as capable of receiving higher truths as the Biblical prophets of antiquity. Nearly a century after her first book, Shinn has proven the endurance of her message.

—Mitch Horowitz

CHAPTER ONE

The Game

Most people consider life a battle, but it is not a battle, it is a game.

It is a game, however, that cannot be played successfully without knowledge of spiritual law, and the Old and New Testaments give the rules of the game with wonderful clarity. Jesus Christ taught that life is a great game of *Giving* and *Receiving*.

"Whatsoever a man soweth that shall he also reap." This means that whatever a person sends out in word or deed, will return to him; what he gives, he will receive— hate for hate; love for love; criticism for criticism.

We are also taught that the imaging faculty of the mind plays a leading part in the game of life. "Keep thy heart (or imagination) with all diligence, for out of it are the issues of life." (Proverbs 4:23) This means that what you image in your mind, sooner or later, externalizes in your life.

To successfully play the game of life you must train the imaging faculty. A person with an imaging faculty disciplined to image only good brings into his life "every righteous desire of his heart"—health, wealth, love, friends, perfect self-expression, and high ideals.

To train the imagination successfully, you must understand the workings of your mind. It has three departments: the *subconscious, conscious*, and *superconscious*. The subconscious is simply power without direction. It is like steam or electricity, and it does what it is directed to do. Whatever you feel deeply or image clearly is impressed upon your subconscious, and carried out in minutest detail.

The conscious mind has been called mortal or carnal mind. It is your ordinary human mind, and it sees life as it *appears to be.* It sees death, disaster, sickness, poverty, and limitation of every kind, which it impresses on your subconscious.

The *superconscious* mind is the God Mind within us all, and is the realm of perfect ideas. In it is the "perfect pattern" spoken of by Plato, *The Divine Design*—for there is a *Divine Design* for each one of us.

There is a place that you are to fill and no one else can fill, something you are to do, that no one else can do.

A perfect picture of this divine plan exists in your *superconscious mind.* It usually flashes across your conscious mind as an unattainable ideal—"something too good to be true." In reality, this is your true destiny (or destination) coming to you from Infinite Intelligence, which is *within you*.

Many people are ignorant of their true destinies. They strive for things and situations that do not belong to them, and would bring only failure and dissatisfaction if attained.

For example, a woman asked me to "speak the word" that she would marry a certain man. (She called him A.B.) I replied that this would be a violation of spiritual law, but that I would speak the word for the *right man*, the "divine selection."

I added, "If A.B. is the right man you can't lose him; and if he isn't, you will receive his equivalent." She saw A.B. frequently but made no headway in their friendship. One evening she said, "You know, for the last week A.B. hasn't seemed so wonderful to me." I replied, "Maybe he is not the divine selection—another man may be the right one."

Soon after, she did meet another man, who fell in love with her at once and who told her she was his ideal. In fact, he said all the things that she had always wished A.B. would say to her.

This illustration shows the law of substitution. A right idea was substituted for a wrong one and, hence, no loss or sacrifice was entailed. Jesus said, "Seek ye first the Kingdom of God and his righteousness; and all these things shall be added unto you," and he said the Kingdom is *within man*.

The Kingdom is the realm of *right ideas*, or the divine pattern, revealed to us by our superconscious mind, or Christ within. In the following chapters we will learn more about the awesome possibilities of this power within us.

Chapter Two

The Law of Prosperity

O ne of the greatest messages given to humanity
through Scripture is that God is man's supply,
and that man can release, *through his spoken
word*, all that is his by divine right. He must, however,
have *perfect faith in his spoken word*.

Isaiah said, "My word shall not return unto me
void, but shall accomplish that where unto it is sent."
Words and thoughts are a tremendous vibratory force,
ever molding man's body and affairs.

But remember, if one asks for success and prepares
for failure, he will get the situation he has prepared for.
A man once asked me to speak the word that a certain debt would be wiped out. I found that he spent his
time planning what he would say to his debtor when he
did not pay his bill, thereby neutralizing my words. He
should have seen himself paying the debt.

We see a wonderful depiction of this in the Bible, relating to three kings in the desert, who were without water for their men and horses. They consulted the prophet Elisha, who gave them this astonishing message: "Thus saith the Lord—Ye shall not see wind, neither shall ye see rain, yet make this valley full of ditches."

You must prepare for the thing you have asked for *when there isn't the slightest sign of it.*

Your adverse thoughts, doubt, and fear surge from the subconscious. They are the "army of the aliens," which must be put to flight. Having made a statement of high spiritual truth, you have challenged the old beliefs in your subconscious, and "error is exposed" to be put out. In fact, a big demonstration is usually preceded by tormenting thoughts. This explains why it is often "darkest before the dawn."

At these times of challenge, you must make your affirmations of truth repeatedly, and rejoice and give thanks that you have already received. "Before ye call I shall answer." This means that "every good and perfect gift" is already yours, awaiting your recognition.

The children of Israel were told that they could have all the land they could see. This is true for each of us. You have only the land within your own mental vision. Every great work, every big accomplishment, has been brought into manifestation through holding to the vision, and often just before the big achievement, comes apparent failure and discouragement.

When the children of Israel reached the "Promised Land" they were afraid to enter, for they said it was filled with giants who made they feel like grasshoppers. This is almost everyone's experience. The one who knows spiritual law, however, is undisturbed by appearance, and rejoices while he is "yet in captivity." He holds to his vision, and gives thanks that the end is accomplished.

CHAPTER THREE

The Power of the Word

A person who knows *the power of the word* becomes very careful of his conversation. He has only to watch the reaction of his words to know that they do "not return void." Through his spoken word man is continually making laws for himself.

I have a friend who often says on the phone, "Do come to see me and have a fine old-fashioned chat." This "old-fashioned chat" means an hour of about five hundred to a thousand destructive words, the principal topics being loss, lack, failure, and sickness.

I reply: "No, thank you, I've had enough old-fashioned chats in my life; they are too expensive. But I will be glad to have a new-fashioned chat, and talk about what we want, not what we don't want."

There is an old saying that man only dares use his words for three purposes: to "heal, bless, or prosper."

What you say of others will be said of you, and what you wish for another, you are wishing for yourself.

Your only true enemies are within. The enlightened person, therefore, endeavors to perfect himself on his neighbor. His work is to send out goodwill and blessings to every being. And the marvelous thing is, if you bless a man he has no power to harm you. *Goodwill produces a great aura of protection about the one who sends it, and "No weapon that is formed against him shall prosper." In other words, love and goodwill destroy the enemies within one's self—therefore, one has no enemies on the external.*

There is peace on earth for him who sends goodwill to man.

CHAPTER FOUR

The Law of Nonresistance

Nothing on earth can resist an absolutely non-resistant person.

The Chinese say that water is the most powerful element because it is perfectly nonresistant. It can wear away a rock, and sweep all that is before it.

Jesus said, "Resist not evil," for He knew, in reality, there is no evil, therefore nothing to resist. Evil has come of man's "vain imagination," or a belief in two powers: good and evil.

There is an old legend that Adam and Eve ate of "Maya the Tree of Illusion," and saw two powers instead of one power, God. *Therefore, evil is a false law that man has made for himself.*

Man's soul is his subconscious mind, and whatever he feels deeply, good or bad, is outpictured by that faithful servant. His body and affairs reflect what he has been picturing. The sick man has pictured his sickness, the poor man, poverty, the rich man, wealth. Children are sensitive and receptive to the thoughts of others about them, and often outpicture the fears of their parents.

A metaphysician once said, "If you do not run your subconscious mind yourself, someone else will run it for you." The man who is centered and established in right thinking, the man who sends out only goodwill, and who is without fear, cannot be *touched or influenced by the negative thoughts of others.*

Some of us are kept in bondage by thoughts of the past. Living in the past is a failure and a violation of spiritual law. The past keeps you blocked. You must bless it and forget it; you should likewise bless the future, knowing that it has in store for you endless joys; but you must live *fully in the now.*

Make this affirmation immediately upon waking: *Thy will be done this day! Today is a day of completion; I give thanks for this perfect day, miracle shall follow miracle, and wonders shall never cease.*

Make this a daily habit—and you *will* see wonders and miracles enter your life.

CHAPTER FIVE

The Law of Karma

The Game of Life is a game of boomerangs. Man's thoughts, deeds, and words return to him, sooner or later, with astounding accuracy.

This is the Law of Karma, which is another way of saying, "Whatsoever a man soweth, that also shall he reap."

The more you know about the Game of Life, the more you are responsible for. Someone with knowledge of Spiritual Law who does not practice it, suffers greatly in consequence. In the Bible, if we read the word Lord as law it will make many passages much clearer. "The fear of the Lord (law) is the beginning of wisdom."

Always remember that *your desires are a tremendous force; they must be directed in the right channels or chaos ensues.*

In demonstrating, the first and most important step is to *ask aright.* Man should always demand only that which is his by *divine right*. We are admonished: "My will be done not thine." And man always gets just what he desires when he *relinquishes personal will*, thereby enabling Infinite Intelligence to work through him. "Stand ye still and see the salvation of the Lord (law)."

A woman came to me in great distress. Her daughter had determined to take a very hazardous trip, and the mother was filled with fear. She had used every argument, had pointed out the dangers, and forbidden her to go. But the daughter became only more rebellious and determined. I told the mother, "You are forcing your personal will upon your daughter, which you have no right to do. Your fear of the trip is only attracting it, for we attract what we fear."

I added, "Let go, and take your mental hands off. *Put it in God's hands, and use this statement*: 'I put this situation in the hands of Infinite Love and Wisdom; if this trip is the Divine plan, I bless it and no longer resist; but if it is not divinely planned, I give thanks that it is now dissolved and dissipated.'"

A day or so later, her daughter told her, "Mother I have given up the trip," and the situation returned to its "native nothingness."

Sometimes our most difficult challenge is that of "standing still." But when we can do that, and turn life over to the Divine Will, events have their perfect outcome.

Chapter Six

Casting the Burden
(Impressing the Subconscious)

When you understand the workings of your mind, your great desire is to find an easy and quick way to impress the subconscious with good; for simply an intellectual knowledge of Truth will not bring results.

I have found that the easiest way is in "casting the burden."

In the fifty-fifth Psalm we are told to "cast thy burden upon the Lord." Many passages in the Bible state that the *battle is God's* not man's, and that man is always to *"stand still"* and *see the Salvation of the Lord.*

That is what Jesus meant when he said, "My yoke is easy and my burden is light." He further said: "Come to me all ye that labor and are heavy laden, and I will give you rest."

This indicates that the superconscious mind (or Christ within) is the department that fights man's battle and relieves him of burdens. We see, therefore, that man violates the law if he carries a burden. And a burden is an adverse thought or condition, and this thought or condition has its root in the subconscious.

It seems almost impossible to make any headway directing the subconscious from the conscious, or reasoning, mind, as the reasoning mind (the intellect) is limited in its conceptions and filled with doubts and fears.

How scientific it then is to cast the burden upon the superconscious mind (or Christ within) where it is "made light," or dissolved into its "native nothingness."

A woman in urgent need of money "made light" upon the Christ within, the superconscious, with this statement: "I cast this burden of lack on the Christ within and I go free to have plenty." The belief in lack was her burden, and as she cast it upon the superconscious, with its belief in plenty, an avalanche of supply resulted.

I knew a woman whose burden was resentment. For years, resentment held her in a state of torment and imprisoned her soul (the subconscious mind). She said: "I cast this resentment on the Christ within and I go free to be loving, harmonious, and happy." The Almighty superconscious flooded the subconscious, and her whole life was changed.

When you "cast the burden," your statement should be made over and over and over, sometimes for hours at a time, silently or audibly, with quietness but determination.

I have noticed in "casting the burden" that after a little while one seems to see clearly. It is impossible to have clear vision while in the throes of the carnal mind. In steadily repeating the affirmation, "I cast this burden on the Christ within and go free," the vision clears, and with it comes a feeling of relief and, sooner or later, *the manifestation of good*.

A student once asked me to explain the "darkness before the dawn." As noted earlier, often before a big demonstration "everything seems to go wrong," and deep depression clouds the consciousness. This means that out of the subconscious are rising doubts and fears of the ages. These old derelicts of the subconscious rise to the surface *to be put out.* It is just then that a man should clap his symbols, like Jehoshaphat, and give thanks that he is saved, even though he seems surrounded by the enemy.

The student continued, "How long must one remain in the dark?" I replied, "Until one *can see in the dark*," and *"Casting the burden enables one to see in the dark."*

In order to impress the subconscious, active faith is essential. Jesus showed active faith when "He commanded the multitude to sit down on the ground," before He gave thanks for the loaves and fishes.

Active faith is the bridge over which man passes to the Promised Land. I will give another example showing how necessary this step is.

A woman I knew had, through misunderstanding, been separated from her husband, whom she loved deeply. He refused all offers of reconciliation. Coming into knowledge of Spiritual Law, she denied the appearance of separation. She made this statement: "There is no separation in Divine Mind, therefore, I cannot be separated from the love and companionship which are mine by divine right."

She showed active faith by arranging a place for him at the table every day, thereby impressing the subconscious with a picture of his return. More than a year passed, but she never wavered, and *one day he walked in.*

The student must remember not to despise the "day of small things." Invariably, before a demonstration come "signs of land." Before Columbus reached America, he saw birds and twigs, which showed him land was near. So it is with a demonstration; but often the student mistakes it for the demonstration itself, and is disappointed.

For example, a woman had "spoken the word" for a set of dishes. Not long afterwards a friend gave her a dish that was old and cracked. She came to me and said, "Well, I asked for a set of dishes, and all I got was a cracked plate."

I replied, "The plate was only 'signs of land.' It shows your dishes are coming—look upon it as birds and twigs." And not long afterward the dishes came.

CHAPTER SEVEN

Love

A woman came to me in deep distress. The man she loved had left her for another women, and said he had never intended to marry her. She was torn with jealousy and resentment, and said she hoped he would suffer as he had made her suffer. She added, "How could he leave me when I loved him so much?"

I replied, "You are not loving that man, you are hating him," and added, "*You can never receive what you have never given. Give a perfect love and you will receive a perfect love.* Perfect yourself on this man. Give him *unselfish* love, demanding nothing in return; do not criticize or condemn, and *bless him wherever he is.*"

I continued, "When you *send out real love*, real love will return to you. Either from this man or his equivalent, for if this man is not the divine selection you will not want him. As you are one with God, you are one with the love that is yours by divine right."

I told her of a brotherhood in India who never said, "Good morning" to each other. They used the words: *"I salute the Divinity in you."* They saluted the divinity in every man, for they *saw only God in every living thing.*

I said, "Salute the divinity in this man, and say, 'I see your divine self only. I see you as God sees you: perfect, made in His image and likeness.'"

She did so—and gradually she grew more poised and began losing her resentment. One morning I received a letter saying, "We are married."

There is an old proverb, "No man is your enemy, no man is your friend, every man is your teacher." This woman's lover was teaching her selfless love.

Suffering is not necessary for man's development; it is the result of violation of spiritual law, but few seem able to rouse themselves from their "soul sleep" without it. When people are happy, they usually become selfish, and automatically the Law of Karma is set in action. Man often suffers loss through lack of appreciation.

No one can attract money, for example, if he despises it. Many people are kept in poverty by saying "money means nothing to me." This is why so many artists are poor. Their contempt for money separates them from it. I remember hearing one artist say of another, "He's no good as an artist; he has money in the bank." This attitude of mind separates man from his supply; you must be in harmony with a thing in order to attract it.

Follow the path of love, and all things are added. For *God is love*—and *God is supply.*

CHAPTER EIGHT

Intuition or Guidance

No accomplishment is too great for the man who knows the power of his word, and who follows his intuitive leads. By the word he sets in action unseen forces, and can rebuild his body or remold his affairs.

It is, therefore, of utmost importance that the student choose the *right words,* and carefully select the affirmation he wishes to catapult into the invisible. He knows that God is his supply, that there is a supply for every demand, and that his spoken word releases this supply. "Ask and ye shall receive."

But it falls to man to make the first move. "Draw nigh to God and He will draw nigh to you."

I am often asked just how to make a demonstration. I reply, "Speak the word and then do nothing until you get a definite lead." Demand the lead, saying, "Infinite Spirit, reveal to me the way, let me know if there is anything for me to do."

The answer will come through intuition (or hunch); a chance remark from someone, or a passage in a book, etc. Intuition is a spiritual faculty and does not explain but simply *points the way*. The answers coming from intuition are sometimes startling in their exactness.

For example, a woman desired a large sum of money. She spoke the words: "Infinite Spirit, open the way for my immediate supply, let all that is mine by divine right now reach me, in great avalanches of abundance." Then she added: "Give me a definite lead, let me know if there is anything for me to do."

The thought came quickly, "Give a certain friend" (who had helped her spiritually) "a hundred dollars." She told her friend, who said, "Wait and get another lead before giving it." So she waited, and that day met a woman who said to her, "I gave someone a dollar today; it was just as much for me as it would be for you to give someone a hundred." This was an unmistakable lead, so she knew she was right in giving the hundred dollars. It was a gift that proved a great investment, for shortly after, a large sum of money came to her in a remarkable way.

Giving opens the way for receiving. In order to create activity in finances, one should give. Tithing, or giving one-tenth of one's income, is an old Jewish custom, and is sure to bring increase. The tenth-part goes forth and returns blessed and multiplied. But the gift or tithe must be given with love and cheerfulness, for "God loveth a cheerful giver." Bills should be paid cheerfully; all money should be sent forth happily and with a blessing.

This attitude of mind makes you a master of money. It obeys you, and your spoken word opens vast reservoirs of wealth.

CHAPTER NINE

Perfect Self-Expression
or the Divine Design

There is for each of us perfect self-expression. *There is a place for you to fill that no one else can fill; something you are to do that no one else can do; it is your destiny.*

Your personal achievement is held as a perfect idea in Divine Mind awaiting your recognition. As the imaging faculty is the creative faculty, it is necessary for you to see the idea before it can manifest.

So, your highest demand is for the *Divine Design of your life.*

You may not have the faintest conception of what it is. There is, possibly, some marvelous talent hidden deep within you.

Your demand should be: *"Infinite Spirit, open the way for the Divine Design of my life to manifest; let the genius within me now be released; let me see clearly the perfect plan."*

Your plan includes health, wealth, love, and perfect self-expression. This is the *square of life*, which brings perfect happiness. When you have made this demand, you may find great changes occurring in your life, for nearly everyone has wandered far from the Divine Design.

Many a genius has struggled for years with the problem of supply, when his spoken word, and faith, would have quickly released the necessary funds. After class one day a man came to me and handed me a cent. He said: "I have just seven cents in the world, and I'm going to give you one; for I have faith in the power of your spoken word. I want you to speak the word for my perfect self-expression and prosperity."

I "spoke the word," and did not see him again until a year later. He came in one day, successful and happy, with a roll of bills in his pocket. He said, "Immediately after you spoke the word, I had a position offered me in a distant city, and am now demonstrating health, happiness, and supply."

Demand definite leads for yourself, and the way will be made easy and successful.

One should not visualize or force a mental picture. When you demand the Divine Design to come into your conscious mind, you will receive flashes of inspiration and begin to see yourself making some great accomplishment. This is the picture, or idea, you must hold without wavering.

The thing you seek is seeking you—*the telephone was seeking Alexander Graham Bell.*

Now, one sure way of blocking your Divine Plan is *anger*. Anger blurs the visions, poisons the blood, is the root of many diseases, and causes wrong decision. It has been called one of the worst "sins" as its reaction is so harmful. The student learns that in metaphysics sin has a much broader meaning than in the old teaching. "Whatsoever is not of faith is of sin."

Fear and worry are deadly sins. They are inverted faith, and through distorted mental pictures, bring to pass the thing one fears. Your work is to drive out these enemies (from the subconscious mind).

You can vanquish fear only by walking up to the thing you are afraid of. When Jehoshaphat and his army prepared to meet the enemy singing, "Praise the Lord, for his mercy endureth forever" they found their enemies had destroyed each other—and there was nothing to fight.

Chapter Ten

Denials and Affirmations

All the good that is to be made manifest in your life is already an accomplished fact in the Divine Mind, and is released through your recognition, or spoken word. So you must be careful to decree that only the Divine Idea be made manifest; for often we decree through our "idle words," bringing failure and misfortune.

Again, it is of the utmost importance to word your demands correctly.

If you a desire home, friend, position, or any other good thing, make the demand for the "divine selection." For example, say: "Infinite Spirit, open the way for my right home, my right friend, my right position. I give thanks *that it now manifests under grace in a perfect way.*"

As you grow in financial consciousness, you should demand that the enormous sums of money, which are yours by divine right, reach you under grace in perfect ways.

It is impossible for you to release more than you think is possible, for you are bound by the limited expectancies of the subconscious. You must enlarge your expectancies in order to receive in a larger way.

The French illustrate this in a legend. A poor man was walking along a road when he met a traveler, who stopped him and said: "My good friend, I see you are poor. Take this gold nugget, sell it, and you will be rich all your days."

The man was overjoyed at his good fortune, and took the nugget home. He immediately found work and became so prosperous that he did not sell the nugget. Years passed, and he became very rich. One day he met a poor man on the road. He stopped him and said: "My good friend, I will give you this gold nugget, which, if you sell it, will make you rich for life." The mendicant took the nugget, had it valued, and found it was only brass. So, we see, the first man became rich through feeling rich, thinking the nugget was gold.

Feeling that a thing is so establishes it in the subconscious. It would not be necessary to make an affirmation more than once if one had perfect faith. One should not plead or supplicate, but give thanks repeatedly that he has received.

The Lord's Prayer is in the form of command and demand: "Give us this day our daily bread, and forgive us our debts as we forgive our debtors," and ends in praise: "For thine is the Kingdom and the Power and the Glory, forever. Amen."

Prayer is command and demand, praises and thanksgiving. The student's work is in making himself believe "with God all things are possible."

Demonstrations often come at the eleventh hour because one then lets go, stops reasoning, and Infinite Intelligence has a chance to work.

I am often asked the difference between *visualizing* and *visioning*. Visualizing is a mental process governed by the reasoning or conscious mind; visioning is a spiritual process governed by intuition, or the superconscious mind. The student should train his mind to receive these flashes of inspiration, and work out the "divine pictures" through definite leads.

When you can say, "I desire only that which God desires for me," your false desires fade from the consciousness, and a new set of blueprints is given to you by the Master Architect, the God within. God's plan transcends the limitation of your reasoning mind, and is always the square of life, containing health, wealth, love, and perfect self-expression.

Turn always to the Christ within. This is your own higher self, made in God's image. This is the self that has never failed, never known sickness or sorrow, was never born, and has never died. It is "the resurrection and the life" within us all.

As you now experience these words, may you be freed from the thing that has held you in bondage, stood between you and your birthright; may you "know the Truth that makes you free"—free to fulfill your destiny, to bring into manifestation the *Divine Design of your life.*

"Be ye transformed by the renewing of your mind."

FLORENCE SCOVEL SHINN was born in Camden, New Jersey, in 1871. She attended the Pennsylvania Academy of Fine Arts, where she met her husband, the realist painter Everett Shinn. She worked for many years as an artist and illustrator of children's literature in New York City before writing her New Thought landmark, *The Game of Life and How to Play It*. Unable to interest New York presses, Shinn published the book herself in 1925. She went on to write three more books: *Your Word is Your Wand,* published in 1928; *The Secret Door to Success*, published in 1940; and *The Power of the Spoken* Word, published posthumously in 1944. Shinn was also a sought-after spiritual lecturer and counselor. She died in New York City in 1940.

MITCH HOROWITZ, who abridged and introduced this volume, is the PEN Award-winning author of books including *Occult America* and *The Miracle Club: How Thoughts Become Reality*. *The Washington Post* says Mitch "treats esoteric ideas and movements with an even-handed intellectual studiousness that is too often lost in today's raised-voice discussions." Follow him @MitchHorowitz.